MOUTHPIECE

Amy Nostbakken & Norah Sadava

MOUTHPIECE

OBERON BOOKS
LONDON

WWW.OBERONBOOKS.COM

First published in 2017 by Coach House Books, Canada

UK edition published in 2018 by Oberon Books Ltd
521 Caledonian Road, London N7 9RH
Tel: +44 (0) 20 7607 3637 / Fax: +44 (0) 20 7607 3629
e-mail: info@oberonbooks.com
www.oberonbooks.com

A catalogue record for this book is available from the British
Library.

PB ISBN: 9781786824394
E ISBN: 9781786824400

Cover photograph by Brooke Wedlock

Printed and bound by 4EDGE Limited, Hockley, Essex, UK.
eBook conversion by CPI Group (UK) Ltd, Croydon, CR0 4YY.

Visit www.oberonbooks.com to read more about all our books and to buy them. You
will also find features, author interviews and news of any author events, and you can
sign up for e-newsletters so that you're always first to hear about our new releases.

Printed on FSC accredited paper

For Janis and Anne

AN INTRODUCTION
by Michele Landsberg

There's nothing more challenging for a vintage feminist today than to convey the kind of constraints we endured before the so-called Second Wave of feminism came along. The passively accepted tyranny of girldom and boydom that regulated every minute detail of life: only girls had flowers on their birthday cake (flowers were feminine); only boys played sports in any organized way; only boys took second helpings and only boys were comfortable in their own skins. As teenagers, we went along with the choking conformity of clothing; we completely accepted rape jokes and the necessity for girls to laugh merrily at them. We girls inhaled division and restriction with every breath and had no more thought of rejecting sexism than of rejecting breathing itself. Our main task was to be pretty and to attract boys; if that same prettiness and attraction led to our deflowering and hence pregnancy, we might as well kill ourselves, so profound was the social humiliation. Of course, we were also despised as 'cockteasers' and accused of leaving boys with the dreaded 'blue balls' if we protected our sacred virginity. Double bind? It was our daily life.

With syncopated movement, song, and spoken (and howled) words, two women – writers and performers Amy Nostbakken and Norah Sadava – summon up this painful past and our present moment.

With astonishing fluidity, they evoke an earlier version of femininity and, simultaneously, their own complicated rejection of it. The lead character(s) in the play – two females, both merged into one and also divided – portray a thirty-something contemporary woman who has just awakened, metaphorically voiceless, to the knowledge of her mother's death and her appalling duty of writing her mother's eulogy for the imminent funeral.

The two voices unite and divide in a riveting duet. The women first appear onstage in a bathtub, comically elided – the legs emerging at one end of the tub do not belong to the woman whose head appears at the other. It's the scene-setting visual joke that prepares us for the complex interplay to come. Both are dressed in plain, white, one-piece bathing suits, making them appear almost more exposed and vulnerable than if they'd been naked.

The bathtub is a useful prop. Twice the women ask men in the audience – in elaborately high-pitched, cooing, cajoling voices and with mincing steps – to move the bathtub for them. A few seconds later, they're hefting it lightly and absent-mindedly by themselves.

As the woman struggles to sum up her mother's life for the compulsory eulogy – a doormat! So perfectly groomed! Always smiling! She never ate a french fry! All those copies of *Vogue* magazine! – she is torn between her filial love and her rejection of her mother's feminine role. It's the perfect way to embody the distance we've come and the distance we still have to go, because, of course, she has soaked up, willy-nilly, so many of her mother's values. It's a universal condition, as we can easily recognize from the groans of recognition and shouts of rueful laughter from the audience.

The fast-paced performance is a perfect blend of singing (eerie fluting, bursts of opera, Bulgarian chants), wisecracks, and wrenching monologue/duologue, along with a precisely choreographed athletic performance that veers from ballet to WrestleMania. Among the sharpest and most painful passages are when the women rapidly exchange the most filthily misogynist bar jokes and the humiliatingly sexist taunts of men on the street.

There's hardly a facet of a modern woman's life left unremarked upon in this deft and searching work. Amy Nostbakken and Norah Sadava have found a wonderfully apt form to express the dilemma of contemporary feminism, without once dipping into academic jargon or movement rhetoric. The whole of our predicament is expressed in the constricted throats of these two women, tightened with grief, fury, and frustration.

The audience carries the unanswered questions with them as they leave with the last line in their ears: 'Huh, huh, huh, we've come so far now and we'll never go back to …'

A NOTE FROM THE CREATORS
by Amy Nostbakken and Norah Sadava

In 2013, we set out to collaborate on a theatre piece about female relationships. Inspired by the writing of Anne Sexton, Sharon Olds, Amy Gerstler, and Sylvia Plath, we wanted to create a work that would investigate the particular nature of the way women relate to one another. We hoped to explore the special closeness that we share: the intimacy of bathing together, crying together, nursing each other, all the while sensing this dark sister of competition and menace living right beside that love. The poets deftly capture the conflicts tangled up in a complicated mess of motherhood, friendship, cycles, birth, death, rebirth, releasing, menstruation, suffocation, cocks, fucking, eating, blood, food, vomit, venom, jealousy – all the forces that are extremely complex and disturbingly familiar. Inspired by these women, we wanted to examine why the darkness exists, and we wanted to make a play about it using the strengths of the female voice.

We began improvising around the subject of female relationships – physically, vocally, using the work of these poets. But day after day we kept gravitating toward stories from our own lives, our friends' lives, our mothers' lives, our own experiences from that very day, headlines about a 'woman's place in society,' the memes, the articles, the enraging ads, the blog posts, the Beyoncé. Everyday realities had us all fired up.

Then the penny dropped. Or rather, after years and years of pressure building behind it, the penny blasted into our faces, knocking off the rose-coloured glasses. Up until that point, if asked what the play was about, we would reply: 'It's about female relationships,' and in that same breath we might add '… but it's not, you know, a feminist play.' As we explored the core of how women relate to one another, questioning how we define ourselves as women, talking about our lives in relation to our mothers' and our mothers' mothers', one truth slapped us hard: we haven't changed as much as we would like to think.

The bullshit is still here. It has just been rearranged and pumped with steroids, and now there is more of it; it is everywhere, and it starts from day one in the womb. *Of course* the play is about feminism, *of course* we are scared to admit it, and *of course* we needed to dig deeper to find out why. Why would we deny being feminists? Why would two supposedly strong, liberated women be reluctant to admit it, to proclaim it? Why were we, women in 2014, still afraid to accept that, in order for change to occur within the society around us, we had to be the ones to change it? Us, right now, today. This idea smashed everything to pieces.

We quickly realized we had to make a play about our own questions, our own realities. From then on our writing came from a more honest place. We tried to peel down to and reveal our deepest and most shameful thoughts, the cognitive dissonance we experience constantly, the layers of internalized male gaze and patriarchal oppression that have been bred into us across many generations, the hypocrisy that we ourselves perpetuate.

This play is a document of our personal journey. We distilled three years of intense conversation into sixty minutes of theatre with some added narrative devices for the purposes of storytelling. This play is a naked, vulnerable, raw set of truths that we have been terrified to expose, and that we have been completely liberated by. The writing, creation, and performance of *Mouthpiece* has changed us both as artists, as activists, and as women. We are grateful the work has led the way, and we are humbled by the great guiding force of so many women before us.

Mouthpiece was first presented as part of Why Not Theatre's riser Project in Toronto, 2015

Created and performed by	Amy Nostbakken and Norah Sadava
Directed by	Amy Nostbakken
Movement direction and dramaturgy by	Orian Michaeli
Lighting Design by	Andre Du Toit
Sound Design by	James Bunton
Music Composition by	Amy Nostbakken

Subsequent Performances

The Theatre Centre, Toronto, April 17–May 3, 2015

Klondike Institute of Art and Culture, Dawson City, Yukon, January 23, 2016

Pivot Festival, Whitehorse, Yukon, January 29–31, 2016

canoe Festival, Edmonton, February 4–6, 2016

Undercurrents Festival, Ottawa, February 10–13, 2016

In The Soil Festival, St. Catharines, Ontario, April 29–30, 2016

Fem Fest, Winnipeg, September 21–23, 2016

Nightwood Theatre at Buddies in Bad Times, Toronto, October 21–November 6, 2016

High Performance Rodeo, Calgary, January 25–29, 2017

The Cultch/PuSh Festival, Vancouver, January 31–February 5, 2017

The Odyssey Theatre, Los Angeles, June 2–3, 2017

Edinburgh Festival Fringe, Edinburgh, Scotland, August 3–27, 2017

Spark Festival at the Belfry Theatre, Victoria, March 13–17, 2018

Nightwood Theatre at Buddies in Bad Times, Toronto, April 11–22, 2018

NOTES ON PERFORMANCE

Movement

The style of movement between the two performers through the entire piece is one of complete familiarity, to the point where you forget there are two. One finishes the other's gesture, moves her foot just as the other steps, bends as the other reaches, all without having to look at one another. Each performer can sense what the other will do before she thinks of it herself. This is especially apparent in the morning ritual and in applying makeup while singing 'All I Need.'

Then of course there is the synchronicity. It needs to be so fine and nuanced that audience members can hardly believe what they are seeing.

For the three eulogy numbers, we discovered, when researching trends in dance from the beginning of the twentieth century until today, that the technical moves themselves have not changed all that much; rather, it is the *way* we perform them that has shifted. Orian Michaeli's choreography takes a core movement sequence and adapts it to suit the small, tight, conservative movements of the 1940s, the wild, messy, liberated vibe of the 1960s, and the sexy/militant Beyoncé-like language of our current day.

As with the narrative of the musical compositions, the subtle layers of meaning in the choreography create a richer and more layered experience for the audience. Even if observers struggle to find words for what they are watching, they feel it somewhere.

Music

The music in *Mouthpiece* reflects the inner state of Cassandra while integrating the history of the female voice into the current world of the play.

For as long as musical composition has been recorded and archived, we know that even when women couldn't speak up, when they couldn't vote, or assert control of their bodies, or be published or perform or direct or defy, they could sing. And they did. They do.

The musical narrative takes the audience on a journey: through a mother's lullaby, a Southern hymn, a Bulgarian chant, an opera duet, Billie Holiday, the Andrews Sisters, Janis Joplin mixed with Tina Turner, Joni Mitchell, and finally a Nicki Minaj/Beyoncé mash-up. These musical inspirations communicate how much progress women have made, all the while slapping us with the reality that we must climb much further.

Then there are the vocal compositions that fit outside what is commonly defined as music: the guttural, the squealings, the glottal stops. We use the parts of our throat we don't normally access to communicate emotions in public, the 'ugly' noises that women seldom hear other women producing. These sounds surface throughout *Mouthpiece*; they are one of the most important aspects of the score and yet are totally open to interpretation. What is the sound of cognitive dissonance? What is the music of a woman unravelling or a penny dropping? What is the sound of the noise in our heads when we resist taking off those rose-coloured glasses? In our experience, the best way to access these noises is not to think too hard about it and let it come intuitively, without censorship.

The play as a whole should be considered a musical score. Every breath, every pause, every moment, contributes to the rhythm and dynamic of the entire piece. When looking at individual sections of the play, always keep in mind how it is contributing to the musicality of the whole. The loud can only be loud because the quiet is quiet, and the pace can only be lightning speed because it also has moments when it slows to a halt.

Transcriptions of the songs are included at the back of this book, in order of appearance. Not included in the notation are dynamics, articulation, and other modes of expression. These should be explored during the process with the performers and the director. Bar lines are in some cases merely a guideline and should be ignored when necessary. Keys can be adjusted to suit the performer's range, if necessary.

The only way to achieve the high level of physical and vocal harmony that exists within this play is hours and days and weeks of practice as a unit. In front of a mirror, humming in the bathtub, hitting a note at the same time at the right pitch over and over. The more time the performers can spend together, both in and out of rehearsals, the better.

Another challenge we found when trying to speak in perfect unison was that the cadence and lilt of natural speech tends to flatten out. To work against this, one performer recorded how she would realistically say a line and we both memorized its melody, like learning a song.

To balance the virtuosic and often poetic relationship, the individual sides of Cassandra's persona should be anything but lyrical. Cassandra is hard. She is cynical. And although choreography exists within each woman's monologues, the performance style is loose, free, totally candid. The key to this performance also lies in Cassandra's relationship to the audience, which is direct, personal, and straightforward. She speaks bluntly with no pretense.

The two parts of Cassandra's brain are their own personalities: unpredictable, undefinable, ever changing. No matter how hard a theatre critic will try to label one as a goody and one as a baddy, one as tame and the other wild, this is simply not the case. Both *left* and *right* parts of the brain change their mind constantly.

Mouthpiece does not propose any answers. Our hope is simply that in voicing our extremely personal truths, ones that we so often keep silent, it will leave an audience asking themselves the same tough questions: Why? Why do I speak this way? Why do I dress this way, shave this way, eat this way, joke this way, have sex this way, react this way … ? What is informing these choices and is it coming from my own set of truths? Am I speaking with my own voice?

Both women are wearing matching white one-piece bathing suits. The performers remain onstage for the duration of the show.

Setting

The stage is bare except for a freestanding bathtub upstage centre and a vintage microphone downstage right. The tub is illuminated.

SCENE 1: THE MORNING

House lights dim, we are in total darkness and complete silence. The women begin to hum a soft melody (score pp. 60–61). After almost three minutes of singing in darkness, lights slowly dawn on the women. WOMAN LEFT is sitting on the inside edge of the tub. WOMAN RIGHT is lying with her legs resting on WOMAN LEFT's lap. The humming ends. WOMAN LEFT is facing the audience, WOMAN RIGHT is looking up. This scene is the game we play with ourselves: wanting to move and wanting to stay put at the same time. All hand gestures are in perfect unison.

WOMAN RIGHT AND WOMAN LEFT: *(In unison.)* My mother always told me that you can cure almost anything with a hot bath.

My mother died last night. Mom died yesterday. I was out at a bar, and she died. So, yesterday I was a daughter, and today I am a motherless child/orphan.

Hi, hi, hi, Aunt Mary? Yeah, it's Mom, she's gone. Sorry, yeah it's just, I'm just, well, I just found out this morning that my mom's passed on, so … My. Mom. Is. Dead. She died. She's not here anymore. If I try to call her, no one will answer the phone.

Both straighten backs. WOMAN LEFT uncrosses legs.

WOMAN RIGHT: *(Overlapping with WOMAN LEFT.)* Dead. Gone. Done. Bit the dust. Sayonara.

WOMAN LEFT: *(Overlapping with WOMAN RIGHT.)* My mother, my mom, is gone. If I knock on her door, no one is gonna come out and offer me a tea.

RIGHT AND LEFT: *(In unison.)* My mom made really nice tea.

RIGHT AND LEFT: *(In unison to audience.)* It's 6:30, it's Wednesday, it's minus fourteen outside. I am a woman. I am not a mother. I'm a writer. I live alone in my own apartment on Palmerston Avenue. I drink coffee – black.

Last night I was at a bar, I drank pale ale and whisky. This morning I woke up, masturbated, checked my messages, and found out that Mom's dead. Tomorrow is the funeral. I have to give the eulogy and this morning … *(Voices overlap creating a synth vocal effect.)* I woke up with no voice/I woke up with no voice/I woke up with no voice/I woke up with no voice/I woke up with no voice.

RIGHT AND LEFT: *(In unison.)* Okay, I gotta get outta the tub now.

WOMAN RIGHT goes to exit tub, WOMAN LEFT hums, and RIGHT joins the humming as they slide down into the tub and position themselves so that only WOMAN LEFT's head is visible at one end of the tub and only WOMAN RIGHT's feet are visible at the other. It looks like there is only one woman lounging in the tub.

LEFT: Okay. One …

RIGHT: I'm gonna pull the plug.

LEFT: Two …

RIGHT: Leap out of the tub.

LEFT: Three …

RIGHT: Dry myself off.

LEFT: Four …

RIGHT: My black shoes.

LEFT: Under the stairs.

RIGHT: I'll wear that grey sweater.

LEFT: Back of the kitchen chair.

RIGHT: My black jacket.

LEFT: Laundry hamper.

WOMAN LEFT starts to get out of tub. RIGHT hums and LEFT joins, sinking back into tub. WOMAN RIGHT climbs to kneeling on edge. As she speaks, she climbs until she is hovering right over WOMAN LEFT.

RIGHT AND LEFT: *(In unison.)* Okay, I'm gonna get out of the tub in five.

RIGHT: I have to get dressed.

LEFT: I have to leave the house.

LEFT AND RIGHT: *(In unison.)* Four.

RIGHT: I have to buy the flowers.

LEFT: I gotta write the eulogy.

LEFT AND RIGHT: *(In unison.)* Three.

RIGHT: I have to pick a casket to bury Mom in.

LEFT AND RIGHT: *(In unison.)* Jumping straight to logistics.

Typical.

Both move to sit on back edge of tub.

LEFT: I have to find a dress for my mom's dead corpse.

LEFT AND RIGHT: *(In unison, with a synchronized gesture of putting hair behind one ear.)* Using blunt language to shield yourself. Typical.

RIGHT: What do you want me to do, cry about it? You want me to curl up in the fetal position?

LEFT: You want me to stop eating?

RIGHT: I don't feel like it. I don't feel anything. I don't have time to cry.

LEFT: I gotta write a eulogy for my mother that I can't even read.

RIGHT AND LEFT: *(Facing audience, in unison.)* 'Cause I got no voice to read it with. Typical. Okay. *(Turning to face each other.)* Two, One!

SCENE 2: HOW TO SPEAK

Lighting shift, as the women sing the lullaby 'Hush My Baby' (pp. 62–63) and exit tub.

RIGHT AND LEFT: *(Singing in unison.)*
> Hush my baby, baby, baby, hush my baby blue,
> I never thought I'd meet a girl as clever as …

WOMAN LEFT comes downstage left and interrupts the song to speak like an excited science lecturer. WOMAN RIGHT sits on front edge of tub, dries herself, and creates a rhythmic breathing to underscore the text.

LEFT: First, we take in some air. If this is gonna work, it's gotta be more air than normal. The diaphragm lowers and the rib cage expands, drawing the air into the throat, down through the windpipe and into the lungs. Then, of course, the process reverses: the diaphragm contracts and the air leaves our lungs. It's under a lot of pressure now. *Pressure, you see, is the fuel of the voice.* With all this *pressure* behind it, the airstream jets back up, past the windpipe, through the throat, and into the mouth. Here, all the resonators are working together: you got the jaw, nose, throat, tongue and teeth, soft palate, hard palate, cheeks, and lips all contorting themselves into different shapes and sizes. You got the back, the abdomen, the legs, the whole body – the entire body is called upon to give birth to just one unique human sound.

WOMAN RIGHT begins to sing.

SCENE 3: MORNING RITUAL

WOMAN LEFT joins WOMAN RIGHT's singing as WOMAN RIGHT comes downstage left. They sing the song 'Father, Father' (pp. 64–65) in the style of a Southern hymn as they perform a choreography of mime and dance that represents a morning bathroom routine: brushing teeth, washing face, shower, creams, and shaving. They move as one, like a well-oiled machine.

LEFT AND RIGHT: *(Singing in unison.)*
    Father, Father, help me now,
    I am fallen, I am drowned, on and on and on.
    Bless the Lord, for I was led astray,
    Take me to the water, wash it away.
    Cleanse my soul, I've stained my name, on and on and on.
    I will promise, Father, on my hand and knees I pray
    To be silent, Father, help me to wash my sins away,
    Help me wash my sins away.

    I give you my breath and give you my lungs,
    Give you my lips and ...

SCENE 4: AUNTIE'S MESSAGE

The women end downstage centre looking forward. WOMAN RIGHT stands slightly in front of WOMAN LEFT.

RIGHT: *(Imitating the sound of a cellphone ringing.)* Vvvvv vvvvvv.

LEFT: Where are you?

RIGHT: Vvvvv vvvvvv.

LEFT: I can't answer you.

RIGHT: Vvvvv vvvvvv.

LEFT: I have no voice!

RIGHT AND LEFT: *(In unison, running hands through their hair.)* Hey! You've reached Cass Hayward – you know what to do. Beep.

WOMAN RIGHT places right hand on WOMAN LEFT's arm. Speaking in unison, with no facial expression, their faces are mask-like.

Hi sweetheart, it's your auntie. You're probably out there getting everything sorted for your mum. You're just like her, you know, taking charge, keeping on top of everything … *(Sigh.)* Well, Dolly, she's not really gone now is she? She's still here watching over us. She'll be there on your wedding day, she'll be there when you have your first baby, and you become a mum yourself. Your old mom will be watching over ya … *(Loudly.)* And she knew you'd find somebody special soon. I'm sure you're gonna say all this better than I can when you speak tomorrow. Anyway, I've nattered on long enough, dear heart. I'll be seeing you. We love ya, bye now.

The 'now' is extended into a long throbbing note that travels into the deeper regions of the voice. WOMAN LEFT pushes WOMAN RIGHT with her hand until RIGHT is standing directly behind WOMAN LEFT.

SCENE 5: GETTING DRESSED

WOMAN RIGHT is standing behind WOMAN LEFT. The text is punctuated with gestures; WOMAN RIGHT mirrors LEFT's movements exactly.

LEFT: What am I gonna wear, black?

RIGHT: Mom would have wanted me to wear black.

LEFT: Mom's dead, so now I can just wear what I want to wear. There's no one left to care what I look like.

RIGHT: Aunt Anne, Aunt Kathy, Moira, Gail, the guys who run the funeral parlour …

LEFT: The guy who moved in downstairs.

RIGHT: Exactly.

LEFT: I just don't care about style, I'm not one of those.

RIGHT: Mom was stylish.

LEFT: Mom didn't have to try, Mom was just effortless. She had this natural ability to//

RIGHT: *(Interrupting.)* //Tonight! The return of the little black dress.

LEFT: Okay, how about this? It's black, it's a dress, it's a classic. Audrey fucking Hepburn//

RIGHT: //Bad week for Hollywood icon Audrey Hepburn. After her second failed suicide attempt, she has suffered yet another miscarriage.

LEFT: Forget dresses, I'll wear a skirt. Hey, look at me, Aunt Gail, I'm Princess Diana!

RIGHT: After finding out about Prince Charles's ten-year affair, Princess Diana died last night at the tragic age of thirty-six.

18

LEFT: No skirts. I'll dress like I always do, pants and a shirt.

RIGHT: Aging actress Diane Keaton is sixty-eight and still single …

LEFT: With a vest.

RIGHT: … And has revealed her five-year battle with bulimia.

LEFT: Why is this so complicated? Mom could just fling her hair up, throw on that old housecoat and suddenly she'd look like she was gracing the cover of *Vogue*.

RIGHT AND LEFT: *(In unison, facing audience, shouting like drill sergeants.) Hello! Look! Glamour! Fashion! Elle! Elle Girl! Modern Beauty! Flare! Flaunt! Allure! Bust! Curve! Shape! Smile! Health! Self! Pink! Dolly! Lucky! Classy! Glitter! Marie Claire!*

Returning to centre stage, side by side.

LEFT: I just don't read those magazines like Mom did.

RIGHT: That shit doesn't affect me.

LEFT: I mean, I read *Vogue*, but it's, like, just for the articles.

RIGHT: Well, there's nothing wrong with caring about fashion, it's another form of self-expression.

LEFT: Exactly.

RIGHT AND LEFT: *(Snapping back into drill sergeant mode.) Cosmo! Cosmo Girl! In Style! Nylon! Pop! Pop Star! Pop Sister! Popteen! Seventeen! Teen Scene! Teen People! YM! O! W! Teen Vogue! Vogue UK! Vogue Paris! Vogue Italy! Vogue India! Vogue China! Vogue Japan! People! Real People! Real Simple!*

WOMAN RIGHT lunges for mic. WOMAN LEFT pulls her back. Flash of light/a sharp sustained beeping sound/fight. This is the first flash of the fight scene at the end of the play.

LEFT: Why do people wear black all the time? I'm not wearing black. There's no black, forget black. I'll just wear this white thing. Mom always said she dreamed of seeing me in a white dress//

WOMAN LEFT's hands are rubbing a V shape at her crotch while WOMAN RIGHT squeezes WOMAN LEFT's breasts. They switch and then travel up her body to begin pulling down her straps.

RIGHT: //America's sexiest sweetheart, Marilyn Monroe, after three divorces, two miscarriages, and an ectopic pregnancy, was found dead last night at the tragic age of thirty-six … The tragic age of thirty-six.

LEFT: Why am I still standing here? I'm not interested in this, I'm beyond this, I'm above this.

RIGHT AND LEFT: *(Singing in unison with gestures.)* I'M A SLAVE/ I'M A VIRGIN/

LEFT: I'm wasting my time. It's all bullshit, it's all meaningless.

RIGHT AND LEFT: *(Singing in unison with gestures.)* It's all about that bass / All the single ladies/ Working for the man every//

All four hands are moving around WOMAN LEFT's face.

RIGHT: //Mom would have hated my shoes.

LEFT: Mom's dead. So I should just be comfortable.

RIGHT: Mom would have told me to wear nylons.

LEFT: My nylons have holes in them.

RIGHT: Well then, I'd better get some new nylons! At least today, I should dress like a woman.

WOMAN RIGHT makes vibrating noise of cellphone. WOMAN LEFT mimes fixing collar, cuffs, buttons.

LEFT: Fine, for Mom.

SCENE 6: BARBARA AND AMANDA MESSAGES

WOMAN LEFT joins vibration noise. LEFT moves behind WOMAN RIGHT and puts her hands on RIGHT's shoulder.

RIGHT AND LEFT: *(In unison with 'mask' faces.)* Beep. *(Beat.)*
Good Morning, Ms. Hayward. This is Barbara calling
again from the Ryan Odette Funeral Home. We still
have not heard from you regarding flowers, a casket, and
arrangements for//Beep. *(New mask.)* Hey, it's me. Oh
Cassandra, I'm so sorry to hear about your mom. Can I do
anything? Pick something up? Cook something? Help you
write the eulogy? Oh, god! Of course not, you're the best
writer. I can't wait to hear what you've written tomorrow.
Oh, god. You're probably working on it right now. Sorry, I
mean, sorry. I'm just … call me back.

SCENE 7: EULOGY ONE

The women exhale and arms float down. WOMAN LEFT turns WOMAN RIGHT to face her, pushes her hair behind her ears and turns her toward the mic. Lighting shifts to mic and WOMAN RIGHT.

RIGHT: Hi, everybody. Friends and family. Dearly beloved, we are gathered here today …

Both gasp, hands float up and snap into 1940s cinema voice. There is a radio effect on the mic.

Ladies and gentlemen, it is so very kind of you all to have made it out here on a chilly afternoon like this one. I'm so very, very grateful. Really, you didn't have to. I know my mother would have been overwhelmed to see so many people gathered here today just for her. *(Counting into music.)* One, Two, One, Two, Three, Four!

RIGHT AND LEFT: *(Singing 'I Knew a Gal,' pp. 66–68, in harmony in Andrews Sisters style with 1930–1950s dance routine.)*
I knew a gal who never complained,
I knew a gal who just gave and gave.
Need a hand, need a smile, need a shoulder for a while?
Just ask Elaine, our gal Elaine.
Woah, woah, woah,
I knew a gal who was the kindest woman I knew,
I knew a gal who would give you the world and offer the moon.
She had grace, she had style, her apple pie would blow your mind.
Our gal Elaine, woo woo, Elaine.

LEFT: *(At mic in Marilyn Monroe voice.)* Yeah, that's right, my mother was a doormat. She lay down for people to walk all over her. Wiping their feet on her mouth, slamming the door in her face, she never said a word, not her entire life. *(Moving mic aside, to audience.)* Are you crying yet? *(Back to*

23

mic and Monroe voice.) And yesterday, she died. My mother is dead. My mother, the dead doormat. I know you're not listening to a single word of this, because nothing I could possibly say in this meek, syrupy voice could be of any value or interest or consequence. But gosh, she sure is tall. Gee, look at her legs. I wonder if she's wearing panties under that white, one-piece//

RIGHT: Okay, what do you want from me?

LEFT: *(Back to normal voice.)* I want you to get out of the house, buy the casket, pick the flowers, and get her dressed.

RIGHT: Fine.

LEFT: Fine.

RIGHT: I'll do it.

LEFT: I'll do it. And I want you to write a three-dimensional eulogy to read tomorrow at Mom's funeral.

SCENE 8: THE BAY

The women sing an opera duet (p. 69) while they lift the tub like a casket and turn it lengthwise. WOMAN LEFT sits on the front of the tub. WOMAN RIGHT sits on the back mirroring WOMAN LEFT's movements and hand gestures exactly.

LEFT: So, I'm walking through the food court of the Eaton Centre on my way to get nylons.

RIGHT: *(As salesperson.)* Excuse me, ma'am, can I get you anything in another size?

LEFT: I'm trying to write this eulogy for my mother, but there's that smell. You know, deep-fried food all around me. And then it hits me.

RIGHT: *(As salesperson.)* Would you like pantyhose, stockings, thigh-highs?

LEFT: I never saw my mother eat a french fry. *(Beat.)* So, now I'm here, hiding. I've locked myself inside the change room in the lingerie department at the Bay. I can't think about nylons right now. 'Cause the thing is …

RIGHT: The thing is …

LEFT: The thing is, I never saw my mother eat a french fry. Do you understand what I'm saying? Not in her entire life did my mom taste fries. She didn't order them because she didn't want to get fat.

RIGHT: *(As salesperson.)* Would you like control tops? Hold-ups? Lace-ups?

LEFT: Shut up! I just need a minute to get my head together.

RIGHT: *(As salesperson.)* Every woman has a figure problem. Slim 'n' Slender is the best way to guard against figure tragedy.

LEFT: My mother was raised wearing girdles, and foundation garments, and those strappy hold-in machines.

RIGHT: *(As salesperson.)* Is your home rose-fresh in every room?

LEFT: She was a perfect mother and a perfect wife and nice, nice, nice all the time. My poor mother, no wonder she was so worried about stupid shit.

RIGHT: *(As salesperson.)* Tame your tummy while you strut your way to success.

LEFT: No wonder she ate cottage cheese.

RIGHT: *(As salesperson.)* Surf gets your whites whiter.

LEFT: No wonder she drank white wine spritzers all the time, and smiled and laughed, laughed and smiled.

RIGHT: *(As salesperson.)* Avoid embarrassing stains, and smile without fear.

LEFT: No wonder her favourite movie was *The Wedding Planner*, *White Wedding* …

Both inhale and slowly slide into the tub as they list movies.

RIGHT AND LEFT: *(In unison.) The Bachelorette, An Unmarried Woman, The Proposal, I Do (But I Don't), A Holiday Engagement, The Five-Year Engagement, 27 Dresses, Something Borrowed, Something New, Made of Honor, Bridesmaids, Bride Wars, Runaway Bride, Father of the Bride, Corpse Bride, Romancing the Bride, Confessions of an American Bride, Bride and Prejudice.*

Women burst back into original position.

LEFT: I fucking love being single, actually! Just do whatever I want, whenever I want.

RIGHT: Even if I do get married, I'll probably have a small wedding, actually more like a big party.

Both take a deep breath; WOMAN LEFT rights herself only to fall back deeper into the tub.

RIGHT AND LEFT: *(In unison.) Rachel Getting Married, Peggy Sue Got Married, American Wedding, My Best Friend's Wedding, My Big Fat Greek Wedding, Polish Wedding, A Wedding, My First Wedding …*

WOMAN RIGHT starts to push WOMAN LEFT's head, then arms, then legs into the tub in order to trade places with her to finally end up sitting at the front.

RIGHT AND LEFT: *(In unison.) The Wedding Date, The Wedding Banquet, The Wedding Dress, The Wedding Singer, Muriel's Wedding, Betsy's Wedding, Monsoon Wedding, Wedding Crashers, Four Weddings and a Funeral, Monster-In-Law, The First Wives Club, Run for Your Wife.*

RIGHT: No wonder Mom was so messed up! It's amazing she even survived all that. Forget nylons. I'm putting down the nylons. I'm just gonna leave the change room, exit the Bay, and get on a streetcar.

WOMAN LEFT starts to make a groaning sound.

RIGHT: Then I'll pick out a casket for my mom. *(She joins in the groaning.)*

SCENE 9: A MOTHER'S VOICE

Lighting shift. WOMAN RIGHT is downstage left speaking as an excited coach or gym teacher. WOMAN LEFT stays sitting on the inside edge of the tub and creates a rhythmic breathing pattern to underscore the text.

RIGHT: A mother's voice acts as a kind of umbilical cord. A sonic bath, an audio-phonic sphere, the first psychic space in which the mother has the opportunity to pass information to her fetus that will help develop its sense of self, its personality, its ego. Now, the maternal voice is louder and more audible than all other voices because it passes not just through the air but through the body, moving from abdominal tissue into amniotic sac via the spine and the pelvic arch. So, with all this physical pressure behind it, the sound waves actually create tiny impressions on the teeny little eardrums and skin. Meaning the voice is actually felt and not just heard.

WOMAN LEFT stops rhythmic breathing.

When a mother speaks she is truly engaging in body-to-body contact with the baby in her womb.

WOMAN RIGHT and LEFT inhale in unison. WOMAN LEFT moves to stand at the front of the tub.

RIGHT AND LEFT: *(In unison as catcaller.)* Hey lady, looking very good from up here!

They look up simultaneously.

LEFT: Hey, thanks!

RIGHT: Go fuck yourself!

SCENE 10: NADIA'S MESSAGE

WOMAN RIGHT rushes to mic. Flash of light/sound/fight as WOMAN LEFT grabs her and pulls her back so they are standing centre stage with mask-like faces.

RIGHT AND LEFT: *(In unison.)* Hi lover, it's Nadia. Babe, I'm so sorry, I don't know what to say really. I'm just so sorry. If, um, it makes you feel any better, Jared just left me. I'm not trying to be selfish at all, it's not about me, it's about you. I just thought that maybe you might want to be with someone else today who's also in a shitty mood. Not that your mood is shitty. Your mood is probably just sad and shocked and lost and so much deeper than, you know, a man leaving you after three years. Anyway, I have, like, nothing else to do today so I'm all yours. I have no pants on, I have some wine, I have some magazines and I love youuu.

'You' is extended into a brief chirping melody. Beat. Both look ahead into a mirror. WOMAN LEFT hums 'All I Need' (pp. 70–71) in the style of Joni Mitchell. WOMAN RIGHT joins. Lyrics are sung simultaneously: the melodies/lyrics are interwoven. The women mime applying makeup – their own and each other's in a simple, intimate choreography of daily actions.

LEFT: *(Singing.)*
I'm on my own, another one is gone,
And I'm left wondering who I was before.

No need to talk, I don't want to cry,
Just need some time, then I'll be fine.

That's all I need, it's all I need,
I'll make it on my own.
That's all I need, it's all I need,
It's where I'll be found.

RIGHT: *(Singing.)*
> I'm on my own, another one is gone,
> I am all alone.
> There's no time for excuses, it's you.
>
> That's all I need, it's all I need,
> Moving, it's all I need, it's all I need,
> It's where I'll be found.

They finish their makeup and continue singing while moving to the tub. They attempt to pick it up and suddenly stop.

LEFT: *(High-pitched, apologetic voice to audience.)* Sorry, I'm really sorry to have to interrupt the show, guys. So, so sorry. If I could just ask for two//

WOMAN RIGHT motions to the technician. House lights are turned on.

Oh! If I could just ask for two volunteers to quickly come up onto the stage please.

RIGHT: Why don't you just pick two?

LEFT: Oh, okay … *(Scans audience and picks a man.)* You.

RIGHT: *(Scans audience and picks a man.)* And you.

LEFT: Thanks so much. If you could just quickly come up on the stage please. *(Motioning to the tub.)* It's just so heavy.

RIGHT: *(Directing the men to either end of the tub.)* So, if you could take that end of the tub and you take this end of the tub. If you can just lift the tub and turn it sideways. Perfect! Now if you could take three steps forward …

LEFT: Super! Now just take two steps back.

RIGHT: Great! Yup, now just put the tub down and turn it onto its side.

LEFT: *(Motioning for the bathtub to be placed on its side to face the audience and pointing to spike tape on stage floor.)* Yep, sorry, on this mark.

RIGHT: Perfect! Thank you so much, you've been so helpful. You can go back to your seats now.

LEFT: Thank you so much, guys.

The men return to their seats and the women continue singing. As they finish the song, WOMAN RIGHT climbs inside and WOMAN LEFT disappears behind the tub.

RIGHT AND LEFT: *(Singing in unison.)*
That's all I need, it's all I need,
It's where I'll be found.

SCENE 11: FUNERAL HOME

Lights change. WOMAN RIGHT is in the fetal position, breathing heavily. She slowly calms her breathing and turns her head to face the audience.

RIGHT: I came here to pick out a casket for my mom. Now, I'm inside this pine box … hiding. Because Barbara wants me to choose. Now. It's just an arbitrary choice. It's not like she'll notice what kind of box she's in. She's dead. But the thing is … the thing is … I just need a minute to think. My mother was more than girdles and cottage cheese. This is the person that I knew the best in the world. I knew her better than anyone else. I'm a writer, for chrissake. I should be able to articulate all this, what she was actually like on the inside. What did she love, what did she actually really love?

Well, she loved me, that's for sure. She loved her records, she loved games. We played a lot of card games. Actually, we started playing them a lot more when she went into the hospital. Same old games. Same rules. No cheating. No way was there cheating with my mother. She was super strict and made you feel like shit if you cheated. Not that she yelled or anything, just quietly disapproved.

WOMAN LEFT's mouth appears through the drain hole in the bathtub.

LEFT: I'm so disappointed in you, Cassandra.

From this point, every time WOMAN RIGHT speaks, she moves around the tub as though she's trying to find a comfortable position.

RIGHT: You know, she used to tell me stories while we played. Same old stories. Same fairytales. She had recited them so many times that she didn't even have to think about it anymore, and anyway she could do twelve things at the same time. It was like kind of her superpower.

LEFT: Once upon a time, there was an old woman who couldn't have any children. Broken-hearted, she went to see the witch …

RIGHT: Let me see if I can remember how the rules of the game go. When using a regular deck, a card is either added or removed, resulting in one unmatchable card. This card is called the 'Old Maid,' and if you have it in your hand at the end of the round, you are the loser.

LEFT: 'Isn't she pretty?' the prince said to his friends …

RIGHT: The other players will then torment you with taunts of 'Old Maid!' until a new hand is dealt.

LEFT: Crying her heart out, and certain that nobody wanted her because she was ugly, Thumbelina left the spider's house …

RIGHT: So if you have the Old Maid in your hand, you must to do everything in your power to get rid of it.

LEFT: There she met the king of the fairies who instantly asked her to marry him.

WOMAN RIGHT now rests comfortably back in the fetal position, having moved all the way around so she lies with her head at the opposite end of the tub just under the drain hole.

RIGHT: In Old Maid everyone wins – except the loser.

LEFT: And they all lived happily ever after. *(Mouth disappears from hole.)*

RIGHT: *(Beat.)* My mother loved games?! What the hell is wrong with me, why can't I write this thing? It's just a stupid eulogy. No, it's my responsibility. It's up to me to reveal the fierce Amazonian warrior woman that she was on the inside – that no one else ever got to see! Why am I so angry?//

LEFT: *(Knocking from behind tub.)* //Excuse me, are you inside there, Ms. Hayward? Um, I'm going to have to ask you to make some kind of decision about your mother's casket.

SCENE 12: SECOND SPEECH

WOMAN RIGHT begins to sing a Motown Heeeya, WOMAN LEFT joins her, rights the tub, and sits in it. WOMAN RIGHT rolls out and walks up to the mic. While in the tub, WOMAN LEFT takes down her hair and tucks her elastic in her bathing suit bra. There is a stadium effect on the mic.

RIGHT: All right, all right, all right, everyone, settle down now! I know you cats have been waiting a long time for this. This chick has come a long way. She's got something important to say, and she's not gonna wait any longer to say it. She's gonna say it now, and she's gonna lay it all out for ya. Ladies and gentlemen, please put your hands together for The Miss Cassandra Hayward!

WOMAN LEFT approaches the mic. WOMAN RIGHT flips WOMAN LEFT's head forward, messes her hair to loosen and fluff it, and pushes her to the mic. WOMAN RIGHT runs to crouch downstage left and watches WOMAN LEFT with anticipation.

LEFT: Hi, everybody. I'm here to speak about Elaine Hayward. Who was my mother. You know, actually Elaine was a strong-willed person. She didn't take any shit from anyone, that's for sure. She lived her life on her own terms. My mother …

Both gasp. Lighting shifts to mic.

… was a fucking rock star!

RIGHT: Yeah.

LEFT: She had a career, she had a kid, she had a divorce, she didn't need a man to get through life.

RIGHT: Yeah, sharper.

LEFT: She worked hard to get where she got.

RIGHT: Give her teeth.

LEFT: She emptied bedpans, she could restart a heart.

RIGHT: Deeper!

LEFT: She wasn't afraid of blood and piss and vomit.

LEFT: Come on, give it to me!

RIGHT: She was fierce, she was a warrior, she had an iron will!

LEFT: Come on, more!

LEFT: She was an iron lady! She was Shera, she was Xena, she was Joan of fucking Arc!

RIGHT: Come on, come on! *(Moving to upstage left, singing, she takes her hair down and puts the elastic in her bathing suit bra.)* Ooh, yeah …

Concert effect on the mic.

LEFT: *(Singing.)*
Mama! Our Elaine. She was my mama, and you're thinking
That you knew her, but she's more than what you're thinking.
Let me tell you 'bout Elaine. Yeah! Our Elaine, ooh!
I know you know my mama gave and gave and gave
But she could also do the taking, yeah!
Don't you know it, yeah!

Both break into full 1960s Tina Turner/Janis Joplin dance routine.

RIGHT AND LEFT: *(Singing 'Mama Mama,' pp. 72–76, in unison and back and forth.)*
Mama mama mama, she was a diva, ooh, she ran the show, ooh!
Mama, ooh, a hungry lion. Ooh, she could bite, ooh!

My momma always told me,
Hush my baby, baby, babe, you've got the power,
You can do what you want, ooh.

36

Yeah, mama, she was strong and tough and fierce and
rough,
She worked it, she could give it, give it, give it, give it,
Give it, give it, wow! Mama! An iron lady! Ooh.
Two, three, four, ooh ya, ooh ya.

My mama was strong, she was tough, she was fierce, she
was rough.
Did it all on her own, yeah. She didn't need no man to
take her by the hand.

Mama was big, she was loud, she was bold, she was proud.
Did it all …

*WOMAN LEFT continues singing on her own wildly, her voice rising in
pitch and volume. RIGHT stops singing and moves into the audience.*

RIGHT: *(From audience.)* Whoa, whoa, whoa! First of all,
lower your voice. We're all out here checking our watches
wondering when the screeching will end. No one wants to
listen to an angry woman. Second of all, who is gonna be
crying over that speech? Where's the tenderness, her soft
spot, her vulnerability? No one can relate to that. You're
making her sound like some kind of heartless …

LEFT: Bitch? *(Beat.)* Butch? *(Beat.)* Dyke? Man-eater! Man-
hater! Ball buster! Ratchet, whore, dog, troll, banshee
woman, fallen woman, nasty woman, feminist! Oh wait, I
got one – cunt!

RIGHT: Okay, enough//

LEFT: *(To audience.)* //You want to know how to get a million
points, ladies? Be a girl, and say the word 'cunt.' Men
at bars and parties love it when girls aren't afraid to say
'cunt.' Because it's sharp and direct like a bullet. They
never expect it to come out of your mouth//

RIGHT: //Nice mouth, Cassandra. We're really listening to you
now.

37

WOMAN RIGHT comes onstage from audience to stand face to face with WOMAN LEFT.

RIGHT AND LEFT: *(In unison.)* This isn't about you, it's about Mom. I know!

LEFT: No one is going to hear me tomorrow anyway.

RIGHT: Not with that voice.

WOMAN LEFT lunges at mic. Flash of light/sound/fight. WOMAN RIGHT grabs WOMAN LEFT and flings her back. WOMAN LEFT comes to rest on the end of the tub. WOMAN RIGHT is downstage left.

SCENE 13: THE POWER OF THE VOICE

Lighting shift. WOMAN RIGHT is donwstage left. WOMAN LEFT creates a fast-paced rhythmic breathing pattern to underscore text. WOMAN RIGHT speaks as if she is a determined straight-A student giving a school presentation.

RIGHT: The sound of the human voice. The sound of the human voice is composed of numerous characteristics, including pitch, tone, accent, and inflection. All of which are dependent on adequate pressure from the lungs. A high-pitched voice signals a small body and submissiveness. In females, it is considered more desirable, more feminine, healthier, younger, and is indicative of higher levels of estrogen. A deep voice, associated with a large larynx, triggers a sense of leadership and power. Breathiness, in turn, softens aggression and is therefore considered to be more approachable. A high rising terminal, also known as uptalk or upspeak, reflects insecurity and a subordinate social status. Deliberately lowering voice pitch in a sex-atypical manner, such as vocal frying, signals uncertainty and weakness.

WOMAN LEFT stops rhythmic breathing.

In conclusion! In conclusion, the ideal female voice is naturally deep to project confidence, breathy to soften aggression, and high-pitched to project a small body size in order to attract a mate.

SCENE 14: THE STREET

Both inhale in unison, then build a pattern with their breathing, one fast, one slow as WOMAN LEFT stands and walks downstage left and WOMAN RIGHT moves downstage right. They walk with their heads down and then sharply open up to become the catcaller.

RIGHT AND LEFT: *(In unison as catcaller, following with their eyes from stage right to stage left.)* Hey, can I say something? You are a beautiful woman, so why don't you give us a smile?

RIGHT: Go fuck yourself!

LEFT: Hey, sure! Why not?

WOMAN LEFT lunges for the mic. Flash of light/sound/fight as WOMAN RIGHT flings WOMAN LEFT to the ground. As WOMAN LEFT stands, they break into an opera duet (pp. 77–78) and face the audience downstage right. During the singing, they each smooth back their hair, pull it up into a ponytail, reach into their swimsuit bras for their hair elastics and use them to hold their hair in place. The opera voices become more intense: higher and staccato. This continues until they arrive at the tub, attempt to pick it up, and then abruptly stop singing and turn to the audience.

LEFT: *(High-pitched, apologetic voice to audience.)* Sorry, I'm really sorry to have to interrupt the show, guys. So, so sorry. If I could just ask for two//

WOMAN RIGHT motions to the technician. House lights are turned on.

Oh! If I could just ask for two volunteers to quickly come up onto the stage please.

RIGHT: Why don't you just pick two?

LEFT: Oh, okay … *(Scans audience and picks the same man as previously chosen.)* You.

RIGHT: *(Scans audience and picks the same man as previously chosen.)* And you.

LEFT: Thanks so much. If you could just quickly come up on the stage please. *(Motioning to the tub.)* It's just so heavy.

RIGHT: *(Directing the men to either end of the tub.)* So, if you could take that end of the tub and you take this end of the tub. If you can just lift the tub and turn it sideways. Perfect! Now if you could take three steps forward …

LEFT: Super! Now just take two steps back.

RIGHT: Perfect! Now turn it all the way around. Keep going … that's right, just put it exactly where you found it.

LEFT: *(Pointing to spike tape on stage floor.)* Yep, sorry, on this mark.

RIGHT: Perfect! Thank you so much, you've been so helpful. You can go back to your seats now.

LEFT: Thanks so much, guys.

The men return to their seats and the women return to their opera singing, immediately pick up the tub effortlessly, turn it and set it down to face the audience vertically. WOMAN LEFT gets into the tub and sits at the back end facing downstage. WOMAN RIGHT is sitting inside the tub facing upstage.

SCENE 15: THE BAR

WOMAN RIGHT mirrors WOMAN LEFT's arm movements. Only the top of RIGHT's head is seen.

LEFT: *(To audience.)* So I've got a pint of stout and a shot of whisky waiting for me up at the bar. But I'm down here, hiding. I've locked myself inside the bathroom of The Communist's Daughter. 'Cause I was walking down the street on my way to the florist and I realized that I can't think about flowers right now, 'cause the thing is …

RIGHT: The thing is …

LEFT: The thing is, I don't like french fries.

RIGHT: She didn't order fries, not in her entire life.

LEFT: I don't like fries, but I order them. I order them so that people see me ordering them and they know that I don't care about getting fat. Do you understand what I'm saying? I don't like french fries, but I order them so that everybody understands for sure that I don't think or care about that stuff, it's beneath me. I don't think or care so hard that I order fries.

RIGHT: Perfect mother, perfect wife. Nice, nice, nice all the time.

LEFT: Mom would sit there with her salad, smiling and swallowing, swallowing and smiling, as Uncle Jake, with his famous sense of humour, would launch into his …

(As Uncle Jake.) A blond, a brunette and a redhead walk into a titty-bar …

RIGHT: *(As catcaller.)* Why don't you give us a smile?

LEFT: *(Leaning back, slowly spreading legs apart.)* Just last night I was upstairs at the bar with my pint of beer, and I wasn't

smiling, or swallowing. *(Grabs WOMAN RIGHT's head and simulates getting a blow job.)* I was the one telling the jokes. The dirtiest, filthiest, most foul-mouthed sex jokes you ever heard. So that everyone knew for sure, I am not one of those.

WOMAN LEFT pushes WOMAN RIGHT's head back away from her.

I'm sitting there in my control-top pantyhose under my skinny jeans under my leather jacket with a french fry in one hand and a shot of whisky in the other, rimmed with my bright red lips.

RIGHT: Who wants another round of shots?!

WOMAN LEFT and WOMAN RIGHT hold two mime shots above their heads and look stage left at imaginary poster.

RIGHT AND LEFT: *(Reading.)* Reebok's plunging sports bra helps you keep your cleavage while you kick ass.

LEFT: *(Both lean forward, cross legs.)* Wait, I got one, I got one, I got one … What is the difference between a woman and a toilet? A toilet doesn't want to cuddle after you've dropped your load in it.

LEFT: And that … that … that has made me hide in here where it smells like piss and bleach and period.

RIGHT: *(As mother.)* Always make sure you change your underwear every day, Cassandra. What if you're hit by a bus?

RIGHT AND LEFT: *(Looking profile stage right and reading in unison.)* The secret to a woman's strength is no secret: Victoria's Secret.

(Looking diagonal stage right and reading.) Strong enough for a man, but made for a woman: Secret antiperspirant.

(Looking ahead and reading.) Bad skin day? We can keep a secret with no-makeup makeup by Cover Girl.

(Looking diagonal stage left.) Tampax discreet wrapper is softer and quieter. Protection you can keep secret.

LEFT: Shut up! I just need a second to get my head together.

RIGHT: *(Knocking, combined with throat-singing/breathing.)* Excuse me, are you gonna be long in there?

LEFT: I don't like french fries.

RIGHT: Lady!

LEFT: I fucking hate french fries.

RIGHT: There's a lineup of people out here!

LEFT: She ordered fries. She didn't like them, but she ordered them.

RIGHT: Joan of fucking Arc.

As she speaks, WOMAN LEFT's hands travel from her knees, up her legs, and over her body until finally ending at her head, pulling her hair back tight.

LEFT: She was a woman. She was not a mother, she was a writer. She lived alone in her own apartment on Palmerston Avenue. She was nothing like her mum …

RIGHT: *(Singing.)* She had grace.

LEFT: She was just like her mum, taking charge, keeping on top of everything – she drank coffee black.

RIGHT: *(Singing.)* She could bite.

LEFT: Rimmed with her bright red lips, she drank pale ale and whisky. She didn't care about getting fat.

RIGHT: Girdles, foundation garments.

LEFT: Underneath her skinny jeans, underneath her leather jacket, she told jokes …

RIGHT: She never said a word, not in her entire life.

LEFT: The dirtiest, filthiest, most foul-mouthed sex jokes you ever heard in your life.

RIGHT: Swallowing and smiling.

LEFT: She knew how to win a million points.

RIGHT: And yesterday *(sitting up to smack rim of tub).*

LEFT: And today *(leaning forward to smack rim of tub).*

RIGHT: She died, the dead doormat.

LEFT: She woke up with no voice.

WOMAN RIGHT starts knocking again, and building a heavy throat-singing/breathing pattern.

RIGHT: Bitch! I know what you're doing in there. You want me to call the cops?

LEFT: *(In male voice.)* Security, we've got a situation. There is a crazy, hysterical, bitching, barking, nagging, whining, moaning, prattling, high-pitched, shrill, overly emotional, angry woman who has locked herself in the bathroom at the Communist's Daughter!

The women exit tub and run downstage.

SCENE 16: THE FLORIST

WOMAN LEFT and WOMAN RIGHT are standing stationary facing the audience downstage left and downstage right. As they speak, they shift their weight in a circular movement so that they are spinning on the spot. With every interrupting thought, they change the direction of their spin.

RIGHT: There are too many types of lilies to choose from. Tiger lilies?

LEFT: No.

RIGHT: Calla lilies?

LEFT: No.

RIGHT: Lilies of the valley?

LEFT: Definitely not.

RIGHT: Carnations make me look cheap//

LEFT: //Cheapo.

RIGHT: She liked carnations//

LEFT: //Cheapo, cheapo.

RIGHT: *(The spinning changes direction.)* Fuck, I forgot to shave my armpits this morning.

LEFT: I can't go pink.

RIGHT: She liked pink.

LEFT: I can't go pink because then everyone at the funeral will think … *(They stop spinning.)* Every word I've ever written, while I was writing it, I was wondering what a man would think when he read it.

RIGHT: *(Spinning.)* Lavender? Cornflowers?

LEFT: *(Stop spinning.)* Not just any man. I picture somebody who a lot of people respect – he's probably a man of few words – and imagine what he's thinking while he's reading it … while I'm writing it.

RIGHT: *(Spinning.)* Sunflowers?

LEFT: God.

RIGHT: Daisies?

LEFT: Too hopeful. Baby's breath? Where the hell is the baby's breath?

Both lean right, moving to left from the waist up as though following a passing salesperson. They try to get her attention.

RIGHT AND LEFT: *(In unison in a loud whisper.)* Excuse me! Excuse me!

LEFT: What are you trying to say, there's no baby's breath?

RIGHT: *(Stop spinning.)* When I'm walking down the street I'm wondering what the men are thinking of me at all times.

LEFT: *(Spinning.)* Geraniums? Orchids?

RIGHT: *(Stop spinning.)* And if there are no men around, I imagine that there are cameras. With men behind the cameras spying on me. I imagine how I look to them – a girl who doesn't even know she's being looked at.

LEFT: *(Spinning.)* Violets? Too sentimental.

RIGHT: *(Stop spinning.)* Even when I'm at home, alone. Maybe he's watching me through the window.

LEFT: When I bend over, do you catch a glimpse of my breast? Does this guitar in my hands make me look sexy? Does this pencil in my mouth remind you of//

Both lean out on the spot, right moving to left.

RIGHT AND LEFT: *(In unison in a whisper.)* //Excuse … excuse
…

RIGHT: *(No spinning.)* When I look at my own body, I imagine
my eyes are his cameras.

RIGHT: *(Spinning.)* It's too hot in here.

LEFT: Mixed bouquets … Mixed bouquets, mixed bouquets
seem safe.

RIGHT AND LEFT: *(In unison.)* Something for everyone.

RIGHT: *(The spinning changes direction.)* I have to go to Mom's
house and pick out a dress for her to be buried in.

LEFT: I have to speak now.

RIGHT AND LEFT: *(Stopping movement for whispered conversation
with salesperson.)* Yes, seven mixed bouquets, please. No, a
funeral. I don't know, I just woke up and it wasn't there.
My mother. No need to apologize. Thanks. Wait, I asked
for seven mixed bouquets, there's only six.

RIGHT: *(Overlapping with WOMAN LEFT.)* Hello, hello, hey, are
you listening? Hey, did you hear me? Hey, hey!

LEFT: *(Overlapping with WOMAN RIGHT.)* Excuse me. Excuse
me, I'm talking to you. Hey, did you hear me? Hey, I'm
talking to you. Hey, hey!

*On the last two 'Hey's, they take a small step forward. Facing
forward, the women break into a powerful Bulgarian-style chant
(p. 79). When it finishes, they snap to lean left.*

RIGHT AND LEFT: *(In unison as catcaller.)* Mmm. Hey, you got
a boyfriend?

RIGHT: *(As catcaller.)* What's a pretty girl like you doing
walking all alone?

LEFT: *(As catcaller.)* Damn, I've got a girlfriend but …

RIGHT AND LEFT: *(As catcaller.)* Wow, I just appreciate your beauty.

RIGHT: *(As catcaller.)* Hey, what's your name?

LEFT: *(As catcaller.)* Cat got your tongue?

RIGHT: *(As catcaller.)* Can I walk with you? Why are you walking so fast?

LEFT: *(As catcaller.)* Why so sad?

RIGHT AND LEFT: *(As catcaller.)* Why don't you give us a smile?

LEFT: Excuse me.

RIGHT: Can I ask you something?

LEFT: Are you married?

RIGHT: You got a boyfriend?

Each sound effect is accompanied with a snap change of body posture.

RIGHT AND LEFT: *(In unison.)* Mmm, schlll, ahhh, damn, tss tss, hey, kiss-kiss, inhale.

SCENE 17: ROXANNE MESSAGE

The women face front, mouths open, searching for something to say. Then they snap into straight backs, chins up, hands on thighs.

RIGHT AND LEFT: *(In unison with 'mask' faces.)* Fuck it. Everyone is telling me not to call you, but fuck them. I'm coming by with a big ol' joint. If you don't answer the door, I'm breaking the window. If you've barred the window, I'm blowing smoke through the mail slot. I am not taking no for an answer. Oh, and I'm bringing that black strappy dress for you to borrow tomorrow. You gotta look hot for these kind of things. Duh. You obviously know that. Oh, and please don't even think about giving a flying fuck what anyone expects you to say tomorrow. You gotta take care of you – *(Barking.)* ooh – ooh – ooh!

SCENE 18: MOM'S HOUSE

The barking 'Ooh, ooh, ooh's become a closed-mouthed rhythmic beat. The women break into the Billie Holiday–style song, 'All I Hear Is You' (pp. 80–82). They push, lift, and move the tub so that it's on a diagonal, step inside it, and slow dance together.

RIGHT AND LEFT: *(Singing in unison.)*
So I talk too fast and I sing too softly now,
Well, I'm gonna sing anyhow, don't tell me what to do.

I was hanging on to my old predictions,
I had some strong convictions,
Now all I hear is you,
Ooh.

I'm trying to sing my song,
But it's hard to hear,
When you're near me, dear,
'Cause all I hear is you,
Ooh.

WOMAN LEFT exits the tub. WOMAN RIGHT follows one position behind.

LEFT: I'm just gonna listen to the other side of this record, then I'll find an outfit for Mom.

She moves to face stage left.

I'm just gonna eat one piece of pie and drink one cup of tea in the tub. Then I'll pick out a dress for Mum.

She moves to sit downstage centre.

I'll just watch the first twenty minutes of *Four Weddings and a Funeral,* then I'll choose the dress.

She moves onto her stomach on the floor upstage right.

I'm only gonna read one copy of *Vogue* from Mom's stack of 1986 to present. Then I'll do the thing.

She walks to upstage left behind the tub with her back to the audience.

I'm gonna do my nails, maybe my toenails, then I'm gonna pick out a dress for Mom to wear to her funeral.

WOMAN RIGHT moves upstage right. The women have their backs to the audience. They spread arms in unison as if opening a closet, inhale loudly as they bring arms down. WOMAN LEFT walks with energy to the mic as WOMAN RIGHT re-enters the tub.

SCENE 19: THIRD SPEECH

WOMAN LEFT is at the mic. WOMAN RIGHT is in the bathtub.

LEFT: *(At mic.)* I am here today to speak about Elaine
Hayward. And what I want to say about her was that I
loved my mother. I forgot to say that, before. So I want to
say that, I want you to know that.

I also want to say that I can't give her eulogy. *(Beat.)* Did
you know, my mother spent her whole life trying to be
liked? She just spent all of her time playing that game.
Trying to be a certain way, trying to sound a certain way.
And it's not her fault 'cause that's all she was ever fed. It's
also not her fault that she was oblivious to the fact that she
was feeding the same thing to me: every lullaby she ever
sang to me, the stories she told, the fairytales, the dolls, the
Disney, her expressions, the old wives' tales, the jokes –
that I know are just jokes. The movies, the magazines, the
romcoms, the sitcoms, the stupid commercials between
sitcoms – that I know are just stupid commercials. Online
pop-up ads and billboards and ads wrapped around
streetcars – it hasn't changed. Nothing has changed. It's
the same shit my mom got, only now it's everywhere!
It's everywhere I go, from all sides, from every angle.
It's inside me! I feel it *right now*. I feel it right now. That
pressure. To be a certain way, to sound a certain way, and
the thing is … the thing is, I am angry that my mother died
a doormat! That she fucking lay down for people to walk
all over her! Slamming the door in her face, wiping their
feet on her mouth. And if I stood up here and I gave you
the nice-nice-nice-mom eulogy, or the sex-bomb eulogy, or
the tough-iron-lady, easy-to-swallow, discreetly-wrapped-
portrait-of-a-woman-tied-up-in-a-nice-tight-neat-little-bow
mom eulogy that you want to hear, that I want to give
you, then I'm lying down right beside her. I can't do it
anymore, I need to stop swallowing and smiling. *We* need
to stop doing that … I wanna say that! I wanna say, get out

of the fucking bathtub, Cassandra, turn off the tv, close the magazine, stand up here, and say something.

RIGHT: *(Beat.)* Why don't I just say all that tomorrow?

LEFT: Yeah, that's a great idea, why don't I just say all that? I would love to just say all that.

WOMAN RIGHT gets out of tub.

I would love to say all of that at my mother's funeral//

WOMAN RIGHT pushes WOMAN LEFT into audience.

RIGHT: //But you're not going to, are you? You can't, because this morning you woke up with no voice, right? You are a healthy, privileged, young, attractive, white, hetero-normal, cis-gendered artist, living off government arts grants in Canada. And you are feeling oppressed.

LEFT: You aren't hearing what I'm saying.

RIGHT: I am hearing what you're saying, I understand you. If you say all that tomorrow, people will think you're preachy and they're not gonna like you. There will probably be some uncomfortable silences. You'll be talked over, ignored, misunderstood. If you say all that, you're not getting laid tomorrow, that's for sure//

LEFT: That's not fair//

RIGHT: //It's not fair when a woman speaks her mind and she's beaten, stripped, dragged by her hair, dragged down the stairs, dragged down the street, lynched, run over with a car, set on fire, mutilated, sold as property, sold for sex, raped, burned with acid, stoned, drowned, missing, murdered, shot in the head, shot in the face … Oh, but I hear you. I hear you. I'm hearing you. We hear you. We all hear you. We've all paid for a ticket to hear you, *you've* got it bad!

RIGHT AND LEFT: *(Face to face with each other, in unison.)* This isn't about Mom, it's about you. *(Beat.)* I know!

(Beat, looking at each other, then at audience.) Wait … I got one, I got one, I got one.

LEFT: What do a woman and a bowling ball have in common?

RIGHT: How many feminists does it take to change a light bulb?

LEFT: No matter how many times you pick them up, stick your fingers in them, and throw them in the gutter, they always come back for more.

RIGHT: Don't be stupid, feminists can't change anything.

LEFT: Why can't Helen Keller drive?

RIGHT: Okay, what's the difference between a boyfriend and a catfish?

LEFT: Because she's a woman!

RIGHT: One is a bottom-feeding, scum-sucking, crap-eatingbottom-feeder, and the other one's a fish.

LEFT: Wait, I got one: what's the best thing about a blowjob?

RIGHT: The sixty seconds of silence! *(Beat.)* See? *(Pointing to anyone laughing in the audience.)* He's laughing, they're listening.

WOMAN LEFT rushes to mic, flash of light/sound/fight as RIGHT throws LEFT to the ground upstage left and rushes to the mic.

So my mother never said a word – not in her entire life.

Both women gasp. WOMAN LEFT grabs the tub with her ass to audience and begins to underscore WOMAN RIGHT with 'ooh's. There is a futuristic pop effect on the mic.

My mother knew she could raise her voice – but she liked to keep things quiet. My mother knew she could travel the world – but she liked to stay at home. It made her feel good.

Both women take their hair down.

She taught me that I can say whatever I want, that I can be whatever I want. She paved the way for me to come up here in my white bathing suit with my pubes hanging out and say these words to you. Mama, this one's for you.

RIGHT AND LEFT: *(Fog machine and flashing lights, dancing and singing 'This Is What the Future Looks Like,' pp. 83–86.)*
You know girls run the world,
You've heard it's all about that bass now,
We're not hte first to say it's our time, it's our day.

You hang off every word
Me and my bitches gotta say now,
We shout out without fear,
You've heard us now, loud and clear.

Huh, huh, this is what the future looks like,
Huh, huh, I am woman, hear me roar,
Huh, huh, huh, we've come so far now and we'll never go back to where we were before.

It's getting hot in here, so hot
I'll take off all my clothes,
I have full agency,
So I can do what I please.
Huh, huh, this is what the future//

WOMAN RIGHT lunges at the mic. Flash of light/sound/fight as LEFT throws her to the ground.

Huh, huh, I am woman, hear me//

WOMAN LEFT lunges at mic. Flash of light/sound/fight as RIGHT throws her to the ground.

Huh, huh, huh, we've come so far now and we'll never go back to//

WOMAN RIGHT lunges at mic. Flash of light/sound.

SCENE 20: FIGHT/FINAL SPEECH

The pulsing light/ringing sound is sustained as a cycle of WOMAN LEFT pulling WOMAN RIGHT off the mic/WOMAN RIGHT pulling LEFT off the mic continues for several minutes. It goes on for too long. WOMAN LEFT then surprises RIGHT when she throws herself on the ground. WOMAN RIGHT watches from the ground for several cycles before she stops WOMAN LEFT. They struggle violently until both women are tangled on the floor, the hand of the other covering each mouth. A sharp flash of light then ends the ringing and the women break apart with backs flat on floor. Beat. Both raise their heads. Slowly, WOMAN LEFT helps RIGHT up. They look at each other, walk to the mic with purpose, look at the audience, look at the mic, take a deep inhale, and then attempt to make a sound – a silent hissing comes out. They take a second, bigger inhale and emit a longer, more audible, but still broken sound. They take a third inhale and emit one sustained note in unison. A recording of the humming that is heard at the top of the show floats in. Then 'Hush My Baby' sneaks in to overlap, followed by recordings of all the music from the show so that the sound is layered on top of the women's sustained note. This montage of sound builds in volume and tension. As the music grows, it drowns out the live voices. The lights dim and the women exit unseen in the darkness. The sound continues to intensify into a crescendo and then suddenly stops. A single spotlight shines on the mic and stays there for two beats. The stage is then left in complete darkness.

The End.

Humming

Amy Nostbakken

Lullaby

Amy Nostbakken

Father Father

Amy Nostbakken

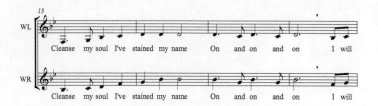

I Knew A Gal

Amy Nostbakken

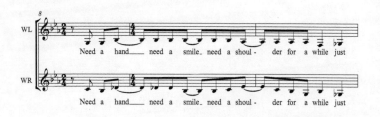

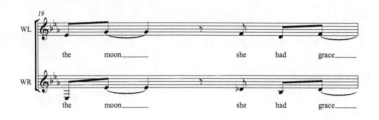

Opera Dirge

Amy Nostbakken

All I Need

Amy Nostbakken

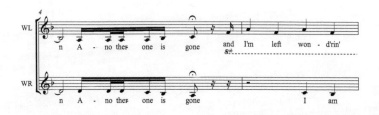

Mama Mama

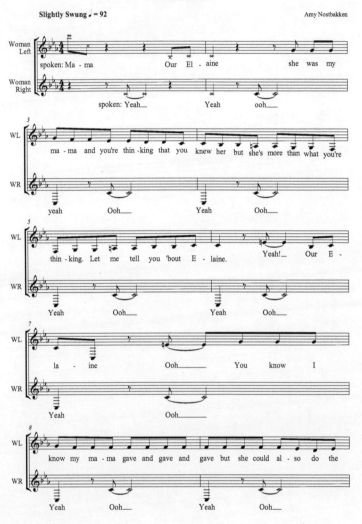

2

73

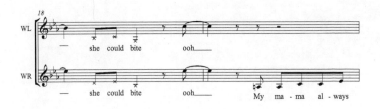

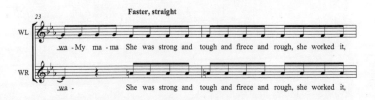

4

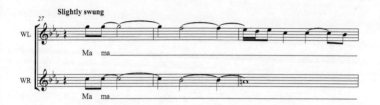

75

Opera Duet

Amy Nostbakken

Bulgarian Chant

Amy Nostbakken

All I Hear Is You

Amy Nostbakken

3

This Is What The Future Looks Like

Amy Nostbakken

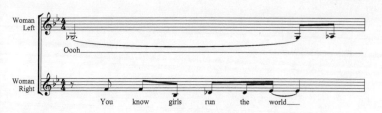

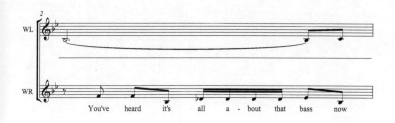

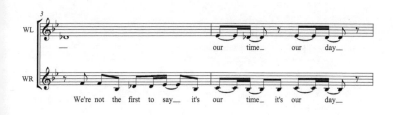

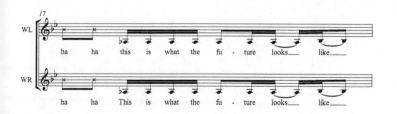

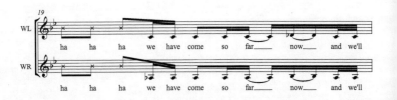

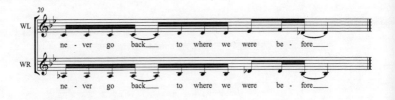

4

Acknowledgments

This play could not have been assembled without the incredible generosity of Linda Goyette, Janis Nostbakken, Rose Plotek, Raha Javanfar, Why Not Theatre, Stone Boat Farm Artists Retreat, and the City of Toronto through the Toronto Arts Council.

Norah Sadava

Co-artistic director of Quote Unquote Collective, is an award-winning Toronto-based performer and playwright with a background in devised physical theatre. A graduate of the MFA program at the Dell'Arte International School of Physical Theatre in Blue Lake, California, she has been involved in the writing and creation of new work with numerous companies, both in Canada and internationally. International credits include The Hinterlands Ensemble (Milwaukee, WI), Mud/Bone Collective (Brooklyn, NY), TeatroIATI (NYC, NY), PunchDrunk (UK/US), and Caravan Stage (Sicily, Italy). In Canada, Norah has assisted in co-creating five-time Dora-nominated *The Double* with Bad New Days (co-produced with the Tarragon Theatre, Toronto), Dora-nominated *The Tale of a T-Shirt* with FIXTPoint Theatre (Toronto), *Bloody Family* with Philip McKee (in association with The Theatre Centre, Toronto), *The Stranger* with DopoLavoro Teatrale (Toronto), *Wildlife* with Events in Real Time (Toronto), and *The Tale of a Town* (London and Ottawa with FIXTPoint Theatre). Currently, Norah is developing Quote Unquote's next show, *Now You See Her*, an all-female rock opera. She also teaches music and movement for performers, and is a certified Yoga instructor.

Amy Nostbakken

Co-artistic director of Quote Unquote Collective and core member of Theatre Ad Infinitum UK. An award-winning playwright, performer, and musician, Amy graduated from Concordia University with a degree in Theatre Studies in 2005 and then trained for two years at L'École Internationale de Théâtre Jacques Lecoq in Paris. She has co-created and composed numerous award-winning productions including Theatre Ad Infinitum's *First Class* (2011), *Ballad of the Burning Star* (2013) and the one-woman show *The Big Smoke*, winner of a 2011 Argus Angel Award, a 2012 Manchester Theatre Award, and 2015 Solo United Festival award in NYC. Most recently Amy composed, performed, and acted as musical director for Theatre Ad Infinitum's highly acclaimed *Bucket List*, which premiered at the 2016 Edinburgh Fringe, and is currently developing Quote Unquote Collective's *Now You See Her*, an all-female rock opera. Amy teaches theatre to adults and young people and runs Quote Unquote Collective's workshops for both amateurs and industry professionals.

WWW.OBERONBOOKS.COM

Follow us on www.twitter.com/@oberonbooks
& www.facebook.com/OberonBooksLondon